THE BIBLE *and the* VIRGIN MARY

PARTICIPANT WORKBOOK

JOURNEY THROUGH SCRIPTURE

Nihil obstat: Reverend James M. Dunfee

Imprimatur: Most Reverend Jeffrey M. Monforton, Bishop of Steubenville
October 16, 2014

Copyright © 2014 St. Paul Center for Biblical Theology. All rights reserved.
Library of Congress Control Number: 2016932836
ISBN: 978-1-941447-53-6

With the exception of short excerpts used in articles and critical reviews, no part of this work may be reproduced, transmitted, or stored in any form whatsoever, printed or electronic, without the prior permission of the publisher.

Some Scripture verses contained herein are from the Catholic Edition of the Revised Standard Version of the Bible, copyright ©1965, 1966 by the Division of Christian Educators of the National Council of the Churches of Christ in the United States of America. Used by permission. All rights reserved.

English translation of the *Catechism of the Catholic Church* for the United States of America, copyright ©1994, United States Catholic Conference, Inc. – Libreria Editrice Vaticana. English translation of the *Catechism of the Catholic Church: Modifications from the Editio Typica* copyright ©1997, United States Catholic Conference, Inc. – Libreria Editrice Vaticana.

Every reasonable effort has been made to determine copyright holders of excerpted materials and to secure permissions as needed. If any copyrighted materials have been inadvertently used in this work without proper credit being given in one form or another, please notify the St. Paul Center in writing so that future printings of this work may be corrected accordingly.

Writers: David Scott, Emily Stimpson, Raquel Lopez, Joan Watson, Matthew Leonard
Media/Print Production: Matthew Leonard, Falling Upwards Productions LLC, Scionka INC, Nate Roberts, Alex Renn
Graphic Design: Alex Renn, Margaret Ryland

Acknowledgement: We sincerely thank all those whose generosity of time, talent and finances made this project possible. Of special note are The Turicchi Family Foundation, the Ruth D. and Wylie Todd Charitable Foundation, and Our Sunday Visitor Institute.

St. Paul Center for Biblical Theology
1468 Parkview Circle
Steubenville, OH 43952

Front Cover image: The Madonna of the Rose (Madonna della rosa).
Photo Credit: Museo del Prado, Madrid, Spain / HIP / Art Resource, NY.

TABLE OF CONTENTS

INTRODUCTION – **WELCOME TO JOURNEY THROUGH SCRIPTURE**..................5

LESSON ONE – **A BIBLICAL INTRODUCTION TO MARY**..............................7

LESSON TWO – **HANDMAID OF THE LORD**....................................15

LESSON THREE – **WEDDING AT CANA, GARDEN IN EDEN**.......................25

LESSON FOUR – **THE NEW EVE**..35

LESSON FIVE – **THE ARK OF THE NEW COVENANT**...........................45

LESSON SIX – **BORN OF A VIRGIN**..55

LESSON SEVEN – **THE PROMISED MOTHER**..................................65

LESSON EIGHT – **MOTHER CROWNED IN GLORY**.............................75

LESSON NINE – **FULL OF GRACE**..85

LESSON TEN – **ALL HOLY**..95

LESSON ELEVEN – **THE ASSUMPTION**.....................................105

LESSON TWELVE – **ALWAYS A MOTHER**....................................115

APPENDIX – **COMMON MARIAN PRAYERS**...................................129

Immaculate Conception. Giovanni Battista Tiepolo (1696-1770)

WELCOME TO JOURNEY THROUGH SCRIPTURE

Journey Through Scripture is the St. Paul Center's dynamic Bible study program designed to help ordinary Catholics grow in their knowledge of the Scriptures while deepening their understanding of the riches of our faith. Distinctively Catholic, Journey Through Scripture reads the Bible from the heart of the Church, engaging both the Old and New Testaments and how they work together. It's grounded in history, yet actively engages topics faced by today's Catholic. More than just an ordinary Bible study, it's biblical catechesis.

This Participant Workbook will serve as your companion for the duration of *The Bible and the Virgin Mary*, one of the studies in the Journey Through Scripture family. It contains summary notes, lesson objectives, review and discussion questions, and more. There's even room to take notes.

At the end of every lesson are suggested readings designed to help you go deeper into the material. These readings come from Scripture, the *Catechism of the Catholic Church*, and *Hail, Holy Queen* by Dr. Scott Hahn, the book upon which this study is based. *Hail, Holy Queen* is available for purchase at www.JourneyThroughScripture.com

So get ready to explore the beauty and riches revealed to us in God's Word through his Church. It's going to change your life!

Queen of Angels. William Bouguereau (1825-1905)

LESSON ONE

A BIBLICAL INTRODUCTION TO MARY

The Madonna of the Rose (Madonna della rosa). Raffaello Sanzio (1483-1520)

The Niccolini-Cowper Madonna, detail. Raffaello Sanzio (1483-1520)

LESSON ONE
A BIBLICAL INTRODUCTION TO MARY

If ignorance of Scripture is ignorance of Christ, as St. Jerome famously stated, then ignorance of Scripture is also ignorance of Mary. This is because "What the Catholic faith believes about Mary is based on what it believes about Christ, and what it teaches about Mary illumines in turn its faith in Christ" (CCC 487). In other words, we can't fully understand Christ without understanding Mary.

Following the interpretive pattern of the authors of Scripture and the Fathers of the Church, *The Bible and the Virgin Mary* examines the role of Mary in salvation history. Through a method called typology (see CCC 128–130) we'll study her role as the New Eve, the Ark of the New Covenant, and the Queen Mother. This study also examines Catholic doctrine with regard to the Blessed Virgin, answering common objections along the way. As a bonus, we'll also explore the Vatican-approved apparitions of Our Lady that have occurred over the last two millennia.

By the end of *The Bible and the Virgin Mary*, you'll understand why Catholics honor Mary as the human person who most perfectly conforms to the image of God. She's an icon of what we are to become. Let's get started!

Madonna of the Rosary. Bartolomé Esteban Murillo (1617-1682)

Lesson 1

 WHAT WE'LL COVER IN LESSON ONE

Introduction: Dr. Scott Hahn, Founder and President of The St. Paul Center for Biblical Theology

Themes Covered

» How to properly read the Bible, particularly passages about Mary
» Review the texts that mention Mary and begin to see the vital nature of her role in helping us get to heaven
» Learn the connection between Jesus, Mary, and the nation of Israel
» Discuss the importance of covenants in understanding the story of salvation history
» See how Mary is the divine "sign" promised by God in the Old Testament
» Overview of the rest of the study

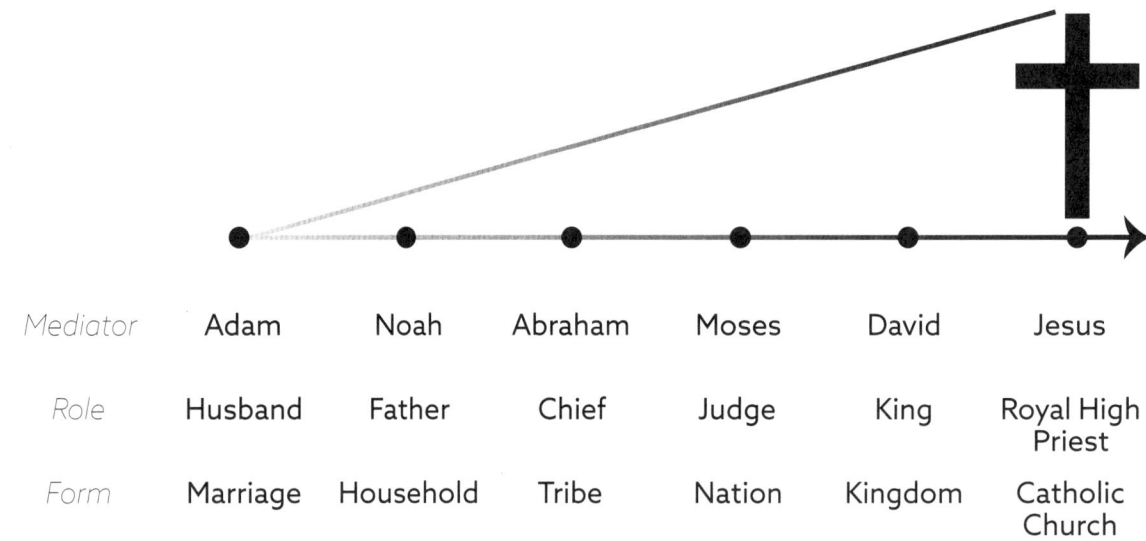

Mediator	Adam	Noah	Abraham	Moses	David	Jesus
Role	Husband	Father	Chief	Judge	King	Royal High Priest
Form	Marriage	Household	Tribe	Nation	Kingdom	Catholic Church

Scripture Verses Read By Cardinal Donald Wuerl In This Lesson

» 2 Timothy 3:16–17
» Matthew 1:18–25
» Matthew 2:6
» Micah 5:2–3

NOTES

"All my own perception of beauty both in majesty and simplicity is founded upon Our Lady."
— J. R. R. Tolkien —

Lesson 1

REVIEW QUESTIONS

1. What does it mean to do a literal or literary reading of the Bible?

2. What is salvation history? What is the place of covenants in salvation history?

3. How does the Gospel of Matthew position Mary at the center of Israel's history? At the center of human history?

4. Why is it important to understand the Old Testament context Matthew assumes when writing his Gospel?

DISCUSSION QUESTIONS

1. The person of Mary has influenced artists, authors, and composers throughout the centuries. Have any of these impacted your devotion or faith life?

2. Why do you think non-Catholics struggle with Catholic teaching about Mary?

3. Have you ever had to defend the Church's teachings about Mary?

4. Have you ever struggled with Catholic teaching about Mary? Have those struggles resolved themselves? If so, how? If not, what questions do you have that still need to be answered?

THIS LESSON'S MEMORY VERSE

> "All Scripture is inspired by God and profitable for teaching, for reproof, for correction, and for training in righteousness, that the man of God may be complete, equipped for every good work."
> 2 Timothy 3:16–17

FOLLOW-UP READING AND PREPARATION FOR THE NEXT LESSON

» *Hail, Holy Queen*, Chapter 1
» Matthew 1
» Luke 1:1–38
» *Catechism of the Catholic Church 484–486, 489*

Additional Study Resources Available at www.StPaulCenter.com

LESSON TWO

HANDMAID OF THE LORD

The Annunciation. Francesco Albani (1578-1660)

The Niccolini-Cowper Madonna, detail. Raffaello Sanzio (1483-1520)

LESSON TWO

HANDMAID OF THE LORD

REVIEW OF THE PREVIOUS LESSON

Mary Of The New Testament

There are only about 15 episodes involving Mary in the New Testament. In order to fully understand them, we need to learn how to read the Scriptures. Doing so requires that we first look at the literal—or "literary"—sense of the texts.

Mary's first appearance in the New Testament comes in its very first chapter, at the end of the long genealogy that opens the Gospel of Matthew. There, she is introduced as "Mary, of whom Jesus was born, who is called Christ" (Mt 1:16). In context, they conclude a genealogy that Matthew has presented for one reason: To demonstrate that Jesus Christ is "the son of David, the son of Abraham" (Mt 1:1). Demonstrating that fact matters to Matthew because of God's covenants with Israel.

The Covenants Of Salvation History

The story of Jesus, and therefore, the story of Mary, cannot be understood apart from the story of Israel. And their story is a story of covenants. Covenants are far more than contracts. A covenant is more binding than a contract. The punishment for violating a covenant is death, not a mere fine or penalty.

Covenants are also much more powerful. Contracts form temporary business partnerships. They involve the exchange of goods and services. Covenants, on the other hand, involve the exchange of persons: They make families.

That is why throughout salvation history, God used covenants to bring men and women into his family. All those covenants foreshadowed the New Covenant of Christ, the covenant through which God would invite all humanity into his Divine Family. God's covenants with Abraham and David, however, have special significance.

Son Of Abraham, Son Of David

Abraham was the founding father of Israel and God promised that through Abraham's descendants all the nations of the earth would be blessed (Gen 22:18). God also promised Abraham that kings would stem from his line (Gen 17:6). Later, God swore an oath to one of those kings, King David, that his kingdom would have no end, that David's son would be God's own son, and that he would reign forever over Israel and all the nations of the world (See 2 Sam 7:12–13; Ps 89:27–28; Ps 132:11–12).

Even after the collapse of the Davidic kingdom 500 years after it began, Israel's prophets still spoke about a "Christ" or a "Messiah," who would liberate Israel's scattered tribes and reunite them in a new and everlasting kingdom that would be a light to the nations (See Is 9:1–7, 49:6, 55:3; Ez 34:23–25, 30, 37:25). This "Christ" would be the son God promised to Abraham and David. Read in context then, the few words that Matthew gives us about Mary positions her at the center of Israel's history: Of her was born the Christ through whom God would fulfill his covenant promises to Abraham and David. Those words also position her at the center of *human* history: The fruit of her womb is the source of the world's salvation.

A Divine Sign

Matthew expects that his readers will hear in the words of the Old Testament prophet Isaiah one of the great promises of salvation history: The promise that God will one day come and dwell with his people (Is 43:5; Ez 37:24–28). The literal meaning of the text here is that Mary is the divine "sign" that God long ago promised to give his people: The sign of God's eternal faithfulness and the sign that God has finally come to bring about the fulfillment of his plan for all of creation.

Handmaid of the Lord

WHAT WE'LL COVER IN LESSON TWO

Marian Apparition: St. John and St. Gregory the Wonderworker

Themes Covered

» The story of the Annunciation
» How Scripture connects Mary with the other great mothers of salvation history like Sarah, Rebekah, and Hannah
» Reflect on how Mary's famous *Magnificat* prayer is connected to the Old Testament
» Introduction to typology and its importance in reading the Bible

Scripture Verses Read By Cardinal Donald Wuerl In This Lesson

» Luke 1:26–38
» 2 Samuel 7:12–16
» Genesis 18:14
» 1 Samuel 1:11–18
» Luke 1:46–55

The Annunciation. Joos van Cleve (1485-1541)

NOTES

"The Church calls her the 'cause of our joy.' ... Why? Because she brings the greatest joy that is Jesus... Pray to Our Lady and say to her what the Church says: *Veni, Precelsa Domina, Maria, tu nos visita.* Lady, thou who art so great, visit us and give us joy."
— Pope Francis —

REVIEW QUESTIONS

1. Why is the manner Gabriel greets Mary important?

2. How does Luke portray Mary as "Daughter Zion"?

3. What Old Testament mother does Mary recall in declaring herself the "Handmaid of the Lord"?

4. What is typology?

5. What are the origins of a typological reading of the Bible?

DISCUSSION QUESTIONS

1. What can you learn about Mary from the stories of the other mothers of salvation history?

2. How does understanding her connection to those women affect your understanding of her?

3. What themes from the Old Testament can we find in Mary's *Magnificat*?

4. How can her prayer of praise inspire and influence our own prayer lives?

5. Had you ever heard of "typology" before this lesson? If so, how has it affected your reading of the Scriptures?

THIS LESSON'S MEMORY VERSE

> "And Mary said, 'My soul magnifies the Lord, and my spirit rejoices in God my Savior, for he has regarded the low estate of his handmaiden. For behold, henceforth all generations will call me blessed.'"
> Luke 1:46-48

PREPARATION FOR THE NEXT LESSON

» *Hail, Holy Queen*, Chapter 2 (pp. 31–36)
» John 1 & 2

Additional Study Resources Available at www.StPaulCenter.com

LESSON THREE

WEDDING AT CANA, GARDEN IN EDEN

Adam and Eve. Lucas Cranach the Elder (1472-1553)

The Niccolini-Cowper Madonna, detail. Raffaello Sanzio (1483-1520)

LESSON THREE
WEDDING AT CANA, GARDEN IN EDEN

REVIEW OF THE PREVIOUS LESSON

The Lord Is With You

Luke, like Matthew, introduces Mary as a virgin betrothed to Joseph, a descendant of David. Luke also tells us that the angel Gabriel greets her with the words, "Hail, full of grace, the Lord is with you." The word translated as "hail"—and which is also sometimes translated as "rejoice"—is the same word that Israel's prophets used to begin prophecies about the promised Messiah and the joy He would bring to God's people (Joel 2:23–24; Zech 9:9). The angel's announcement in Luke seems to be drawn almost word for word from a prophecy of Zephaniah's (3:14–18). Luke seems to be depicting Mary as Daughter Zion, the representative of her people called to rejoice because God has come into her midst.

Son Of The Most High

Luke's account also tells us that Mary's Son will be the "Son of the Most High" and will be given "the throne of David his Father." Importantly, in 2 Samuel 7, God swore to David that his son would be "a son to me." Likewise, Gabriel promises Mary that her Son will be the "Son of the Most High" (See Mk 5:7, Lk 1:35, and 8:28). God also swore to David that his son would rule on David's throne forever, while Gabriel promises Mary that her Son will be seated on "the throne of David his father…forever."

Handmaid Of The Lord

At the conclusion of Luke's account, Mary asks how she, being a virgin, will conceive the child. Gabriel replies: "For with God, nothing will be impossible." An angel spoke almost those exact words to Sarah, Abraham's wife. By using those words, Luke shows us that Mary, like Sarah, is being called to bear the Son of God's covenant promise. Those words also connect Mary to all the other miraculous births in salvation history, including Hannah, the mother of Samuel, the priest and prophet who anointed David king of Israel. Five times in one passage, Hannah described herself as the Lord's "maidservant." In presenting herself as the "handmaid of the Lord" Mary recalls Hannah and her oath. Luke draws the connection between Mary and Hannah even more clearly in his account of the Visitation. When Mary goes to visit her cousin Elizabeth, she responds to Elizabeth's greeting with a song of praise that closely resembles the prayer Hannah prayed after she conceived and bore a son.

Luke demonstrates that Jesus is the last and greatest of these births and that Mary is the greatest mother of salvation history. She is the woman who all the other great mothers of the Old Testament merely foreshadowed.

Typology

Doing this type of literary reading gives us knowledge of historical truth: Jesus was born through the Holy Spirit to a virgin named Mary. But this historical truth also conveys a divine meaning. Matthew and Luke's accounts assume the existence of a divine plan, in which the covenant oaths God swore to Abraham and David are meant to find their ultimate fulfillment in the coming of Christ. The evangelists want to show the unity between the Old and New Testaments. This way of reading and writing is broadly known as typology. Typology connects the persons, places, and events of the Old Testament to the persons, places, and events of the New Testament. It studies how God's works in the Old Covenant prefigure what He accomplished through Christ in the New Covenant (CCC 128).

Jesus himself taught the Apostles to understand Him by using typology in their reading of the Scriptures. Even in Jesus' day, however, this way of reading the Scriptures was nothing new. In the Old Testament, we often find typology used to prepare Israel for its coming Savior. Isaiah, for example, spoke of a new creation and a "new exodus" (Is 11:15–16, 65:17). The New Testament writers saw each of these great "types" fulfilled in the New Covenant of Jesus. Jesus was the "New Adam" (Rom 5:14). His cross and resurrection mark a new exodus from sin into glory (Lk 9:31), and His Church is the New Jerusalem and the New Kingdom of David (Gal 4:26; Acts 1:6–9; 1 Pet 2:9; Rev 1:6).

Typology also illuminates our understanding of Mary. The New Testament writers saw her as the New Eve, the Ark of the New Covenant, and the new Queen Mother of the Kingdom of God. When we understand how the writers use typology, we find that Mary is depicted as mysteriously inseparable from the saving mission of her Son.

Paradise Landscape of Creation of the Animals. Jan Brueghel the Younger (1601-1678)

Lesson 3

WHAT WE'LL COVER IN LESSON THREE

Marian Apparition: Our Lady of Guadalupe

Themes Covered

» The Wedding at Cana
» The relationship between the Creation account in Genesis and the beginning of the Gospel of John
» The meaning of the mysterious "third day" in John
» Jesus' role as the New Adam
» Answers to those who say Jesus scolds Mary at Cana
» Response to the accusation that Jesus insults Mary in Matthew 12:46–50

Scripture Verses Read By Cardinal Donald Wuerl In This Lesson

» John 2:1–11
» Exodus 31:16–17

The Marriage at Cana. Paolo Callari ('Veronese', 1528-1588)

NOTES

"Let those who think that the Church pays too much attention to Mary give heed to the fact that Our Blessed Lord Himself gave ten times as much of His life to her as He gave to His Apostles."
— Archbishop Fulton J. Sheen —
(*The World's First Love: Mary Mother of God*)

Lesson 3

REVIEW QUESTIONS

1. What parallels does John use in the first chapter of his Gospel to show that the coming of Jesus is a "new creation"?

2. On what day of John's new creation does Mary appear?

3. What are some parallels between Christ and Adam?

4. When Jesus says, "O Woman, what have you to do with me?" is He scolding his mother? Explain your answer.

DISCUSSION QUESTIONS

1. Why do you think Mary first approached Jesus about the shortage of wine? Similarly, why do you think she gave the instructions to the servants that she did? What do those two things tell us about her?

2. Is it reasonable to think that Jesus would ever be disrespectful to his mother? Why or why not?

THIS LESSON'S MEMORY VERSE

> "Do whatever he tells you."
> John 2:5

PREPARATION FOR THE NEXT LESSON

» *Hail, Holy Queen*, Chapter 2 (pp.36–45)
» Genesis 2:18–23
» Hosea 2:16–23
» *Catechism of the Catholic Church* 411

Additional Study Resources Available at www.StPaulCenter.com

LESSON FOUR

THE NEW EVE

Madonna of the Pilgrims. Michelangelo Merisi ('Caravaggio', 1573-1610)

The Niccolini-Cowper Madonna, detail. Raffaello Sanzio (1483-1520)

LESSON FOUR

THE NEW EVE

REVIEW OF THE PREVIOUS LESSON

A New Creation

The Cana story— found in John 2:1–11—marks the conclusion of a series of events that began in John's first chapter. John begins his Gospel with a kind of recapping of the creation story found in the Bible's first book.

Moreover, just as Genesis begins by telling us about what happens on each of the seven days of creation, John narrates an account of a new creation week. He does this with a Genesis-like repetition of the words "the next day."

The point of this seven-day structure is to show us that Jesus' coming marks a new creation (See Jn 1:12, 29–34; 3:5). Importantly, on the seventh day of this new creation Mary makes her appearance. This is fitting because the ancient Jewish rabbis believed Adam met his bride Eve on the seventh day. It's also important that in Genesis, the seventh day is the pinnacle of creation, instituted as an everlasting token of God's perpetual covenant with creation (Ex 31:16–17). John describes Jesus' miracle as the beginning of his "signs." The word used for "signs," in Greek, is the same as the word used for "token" in Exodus. That tells us that the seventh day in John's account is the new Sabbath. It is the sign of the new creation and the New Covenant. Moreover, Mary's presence tells us that she is part of the "sign."

The New Adam

For John, as for the other writers of the New Testament, Christ is the New Adam. He is the second man come to undo the damage done by the first. John also understood that if there was a New Adam, there needed to be a New Eve. In his Gospel, he shows her to us. In the creation story, only the name of God is spoken. The first man and the first woman are not identified by name, but simply as "the man" and "the woman." The same is true of the Cana story. Only Jesus is referred to by name. Mary never is. John refers to her as "the mother of Jesus" and Jesus calls her "woman." This is another indicator that John intends us to find a deeper symbolic connection between what happens at Cana and the Genesis story.

Scolding Mary?

That deeper symbolism helps render understandable one of the more difficult passages in John: Jesus' response to Mary when she informs Him about the shortage of wine. The words Jesus uses (literally "what to me and you") were a figure of speech common in the Greek and Hebrew of His day, which, among other things, can show the consent of one party to another, which fits the context of the Cana story.

There is no evidence anywhere in John or the rest of the New Testament to suggest that Jesus felt any hostility towards his mother. Jesus was without sin. Accordingly, He was faithful to the fourth commandment and obeyed his mother and father (Heb 4:15; Lk 2:51). There also isn't any evidence in the Cana episode that implies separation or tension between Mary and Jesus. Four times in the story's mere twelve verses, she is referred to as "the mother of Jesus"—words which link her closely to her Son. Perhaps the best evidence for what Jesus meant is found in Mary's reaction to His words. She turns to the servants and says, "Do whatever he tells you." She doesn't think his words are dismissive; she expects Him to respond to her implied request. And He does.

Marriage at Cana. Giotto di Bondone (1270-1337)

The New Eve

🎬 WHAT WE'LL COVER IN LESSON FOUR

Marian Apparition: Our Lady of the Miraculous Medal

Themes Covered

» Answer those who say Jesus insults Mary at Cana
» Connect the "woman" of Genesis, Revelation, and Cana
» Understand why the Church Fathers refer to Mary as the "New Eve"
» Discover who the true Bridegroom and Bride are at Cana

Scripture Verses Read By Cardinal Donald Wuerl In This Lesson

» Genesis 2:23
» Revelation 12:1–8
» Genesis 3:15
» John 2:11
» Hosea 2:20–21
» Amos 9:13–14
» Revelation 21:1

Virgin of the Apocalypse. Miguel Cabrera (1695-1768)

NOTES

"The knot of Eve's disobedience was loosed by the obedience of Mary. The knot which the virgin Eve tied by her unbelief, the Virgin Mary opened by her belief."
— St Irenaeus —
(*Adv. haereses* 3:22)

REVIEW QUESTIONS

1. What does Jesus mean in addressing his mother as "woman"?

2. Who does Revelation tell us are the other offspring of the woman?

3. How does Mary as the "New Eve" reverse the work of the first Eve?

4. How does the wedding feast of Cana introduce Jesus as the new Bridegroom?

Lesson 4

DISCUSSION QUESTIONS

1. How does seeing Mary as the New Eve change your understanding of her?

2. God uses intimate marital language to describe our relationship with Him. Christ came as the Bridegroom. What does this say to you about God's love? Why do you think He speaks this way?

3. Throughout her life, how does Mary, as Daughter Zion, echo Israel's covenant vow, "All that the Lord has spoken, we will do"?

4. In your daily life, how can you obey the command to fill the jars "to the brim"?

THIS LESSON'S MEMORY VERSE

"I will put enmity between you and the woman, and between your seed and her seed; he shall bruise your head, and you shall bruise his heel."
Genesis 3:15

PREPARATION FOR THE NEXT LESSON

- » *Hail, Holy Queen*, Chapter 3 (pp. 49–67)
- » Exodus 25:1–22
- » Exodus 40:16–38
- » Revelation 11:19–12:2
- » *Catechism of the Catholic Church* 717

Additional Study Resources Available at www.StPaulCenter.com

LESSON FIVE

THE ARK OF THE NEW COVENANT

King David bearing the Ark of the Covenant into Jerusalem. Anonymous, 16th century artist, Umbrian School

The Niccolini-Cowper Madonna, detail. Raffaello Sanzio (1483-1520)

LESSON FIVE

THE ARK OF THE NEW COVENANT

REVIEW OF THE PREVIOUS LESSON

"Woman"

By looking closely at the literal meaning of the Wedding at Cana account, we can see that Jesus didn't intend to distance himself from his mother. But what did He intend? The key to discovering that lies in the way Jesus addressed his mother—as "Woman." Jesus often addresses women that way in the Scriptures. In every instance, He is being polite and respectful to those women (See Mt 15:28; Lk 13:12; Jn 4:21, 8:10, 20:13). It is unusual, however, for Jesus to address his mother that way. Nowhere else in either the Bible or the literature of that time is there an example of a son calling his mother "woman." This suggests that the word, as it's used here, has symbolic value. That idea gets further support from the fact that "Woman" is the only way Jesus addresses Mary in John's Gospel (See Jn 19:26).

The "Woman" Of Genesis And Revelation

Here again, we need to read this passage in light of John's framework of a new creation. In the first creation, "woman" was the name Adam gave Eve. And in the second creation, the new creation depicted by John in his Gospel, "woman" is the name Jesus gives Mary. A "woman" also figures prominently in another one of the books written by John, the Book of Revelation. As in John's Gospel, the Book of Genesis lies behind the scene depicted in Revelation 12. By comparing the promise God made in Genesis 3:15 with the dramatic fulfillment of that promise played out in Revelation 12, we can see that the "woman" depicted in both is the "woman" we meet in Cana—Mary.

The New Eve

Both Revelation and Cana share the same "back story": The creation story from Genesis. In both Revelation and Cana, Mary is called "woman" and in both is described as the Mother of Jesus, the Messiah. It's also important to note that she is associated with Jesus' other disciples. Through setting up those parallels, John depicts Mary as the New Eve. He shows us that just as Adam was a type of Christ, so too was Eve a type of Mary. The original mother of man foreshadowed and illuminated the role the mother of Jesus would play in salvation history. And at Cana, the New Eve radically reverses the decision of the first Eve.

The Messiah's Wedding

Once we recognize Jesus as the New Adam and Mary as the New Eve, we can also recognize the wedding at Cana as a sign of the New Covenant. As the Sabbath was the sign of God's first covenant with creation, the wedding feast at Cana—with its faithful servants and miraculous abundance of wine—is the sign of God's New Covenant with creation. In the first covenant, we witness the marital union of a man and a woman—Adam and Eve. And in the New Covenant, we have a man and a woman present at a wedding. Mary, of course, is Jesus' mother, not his bride. But as the "woman," Mary becomes the locus of a host of biblical symbols and expectations. She is, simultaneously: A daughter of Israel, the mother of the new people of God, and the bride of God, the one who conceives and bears his Son. That Son is also the heavenly Bridegroom, come to fulfill his promise to wed his people in a new and everlasting covenant.

The Promised Bridegroom

We see this promise of "messianic nuptials" in the writings of the prophets, in certain Psalms, and in other Old Testament writings like the Song of Solomon (Jer 2; Ezek 16:32; Is 54:4–8; Hos 2:20–21). In Hosea and elsewhere, the messianic blessings of the New Covenant are accompanied or symbolized by "new wine" (See also Joel 2:19, 24; Zech 9:16–17, 10:7; Is 25:6; Amos 9:13–14). That same type of imagery appears in the Song of Solomon, which symbolically depicts God's wedding to his people (See 1:2, 4; 4:10; 5:1; 7:9; 8:2).

At Cana then, John presents Jesus as the promised Bridegroom, the one who will provide new wine at the wedding feast of the New Covenant. Again, our interpretation is helped by looking at John's Revelation, which concludes with the "wedding feast of the Lamb," the marriage supper celebrating the union between Christ and his bride, the Church (see Rev 19:9; 21:9; 22:17). There too, this feast marks the pinnacle of a new creation. Likewise at Cana, John reveals that Mary is the "bride" of the New Adam, the mother of the new creation.

Virgin of the Immaculate Conception. Anonymous, 17th century artist

Lesson 5

WHAT WE'LL COVER IN LESSON FIVE

Marian Apparition: Our Lady of La Salette

Themes Covered

» The background of the original Ark of the Covenant in the Old Testament
» Luke's parallels between Mary and the Ark of the Covenant
» Mary as the Ark of the New Covenant

Scripture Verses Read By Cardinal Donald Wuerl In This Lesson

» Numbers 10:33
» Joshua 3:3–4
» 2 Maccabees 2:4–5
» 2 Maccabees 2:6–8
» Revelation 11:19
» Revelation 12:1–2

The Crossing of the Ark through the Jordan River. Juan Montero de Rojas (1613-1683)

NOTES

"The prophet David danced before the Ark. Now what else should we say the Ark was but holy Mary? The Ark bore within it the tables of the Testament, but Mary bore the Heir of the same Testament itself. The former contained in it the Law, the latter the Gospel. The one had the voice of God, the other His Word. The Ark, indeed, was radiant within and without with the glitter of gold, but holy Mary shone within and without with the splendor of virginity. The one was adorned with earthly gold, the other with heavenly."
— St. Ambrose —
(*Serm. xlii. 6, Int. Opp.*)

REVIEW QUESTIONS

1. What is the significance of Gabriel using the word "overshadow" when replying to Mary's question?

2. What important objects did the Ark of the Covenant contain?

3. According to Jeremiah, when would the Ark of the Covenant be seen again?

4. Name at least three parallels between the Ark of the Covenant and the Blessed Virgin Mary.

DISCUSSION QUESTIONS

1. What does the ancient Israelites' regard for the Ark of the Covenant tell us about the regard we should have for the Blessed Virgin Mary?

2. Did recognizing that there were no chapter divisions in the Book of Revelation change the way you read Chapter 11 and 12?

3. What do the first chapters of Luke reveal to us about Mary's character?

4. The Ark of the Covenant accompanied the Israelites in the desert, helped them in battle, and marched before them into the Promised Land. How does Mary, the New Ark, fulfill these types in our own lives?

THIS LESSON'S MEMORY VERSE

> "The Holy Spirit will come upon you, and the power of the Most High will overshadow you."
> Luke 1:35

PREPARATION FOR THE NEXT LESSON

- » *Hail, Holy Queen,* Chapter 5 (pp. 89–113)
- » Matthew 1:18–25
- » Matthew 12:46–50
- » *Catechism of the Catholic Church* 88–90, 496–501

Additional Study Resources Available at www.StPaulCenter.com

LESSON SIX

BORN OF A VIRGIN

'The Holy Family', 1740s. Pompeo Batoni (1708-1787)

The Niccolini-Cowper Madonna, detail. Raffaello Sanzio (1483-1520)

LESSON SIX

BORN OF A VIRGIN

℘

REVIEW OF THE PREVIOUS LESSON

How Can This Be?

The Gospel of Luke often uses parallels in words and images regarding Mary. We see this at the Annunciation, when the angel Gabriel tells Mary that she will bear a Son. When she hears the news, Mary is surprised and asks, "How can this be, since I have no husband?" (Lk 1:34). Gabriel's reply is "The Holy Spirit will come upon you, and the power of the Most High will overshadow you" (Lk 1:35).

The key parallel here is the word translated as "overshadow." That word is very rare in the New Testament and it always indicates the transformative presence of God. Luke is referencing a passage in Exodus from the Greek translation of the Old Testament in which Moses placed the Ark of the Covenant in the great tent that was to be God's dwelling-place among his people. In the Greek version of the Old Testament, the word translated in Exodus 40:34–35 as "abode upon" is the same as the word translated in Luke's Gospel as "overshadowed." By using that word there, Luke tells us that the power of God will overshadow Mary, just as the power of God overshadowed the Ark of the Covenant in the Israelites' tabernacle.

The First Ark

The Ark described in Exodus was the dwelling place of God, containing within it the tablets of the Law (the 10 Commandments), a sample of the manna that fed the Israelites in the desert, and the rod of Aaron, Israel's first high priest. It signified God's presence among them (Num

10:33). When Israel was settled in the Promised Land and David became king, he moved the Ark to Jerusalem. Eventually, however, his Kingdom broke apart and was destroyed. The prophet Jeremiah had warned the people of their impending fate. But he also had promised them that God would gather them back together in a New Covenant and a new kingdom. With that day in mind, Jeremiah hid the Ark on Mount Nebo shortly after the kingdom fell in 586 BC. After that, he foretold that the Ark would not be seen until the time when God showed his mercy and gathered his people together again (2 Macc 2:4–8).

The Ark Of The New Covenant

In Luke's account of the Visitation, he repeatedly uses words and phrases about the Ark of the Covenant from the Old Testament to drive home the point that Mary is the Ark of the New Covenant, implying that the time of which Jeremiah foretold had come. Like Luke, the Apostle John recounts a vision he had in heaven that included a vision of the Ark in the book of Revelation. When the first Christians—most of whom were Jewish—heard John's vision, they would have paid attention. If the Ark had been seen, that meant the time they had been waiting for had come. They would have wanted more details about it. But, instead, John describes a woman.

Unlike modern Bibles, there were no chapter divisions in John's day. He went straight from the reference to the Ark in Revelation 11:19 to the description of the woman in Revelation 12:1 without a break. In John's vision, the Ark of the Covenant is the "woman clothed with the sun," a woman who "brought forth a male child, one who is to rule all the nations with a rod of iron, but her child was caught up to God and to his throne" (Rev 12:2). In John's vision, the Ark of the Covenant is Mary, the Mother of Christ.

Within The Ark

Why do John and Luke ascribe such a role to a woman? To start with, the Ark of the Covenant was the sign of God's real presence among his people. In Jesus Christ, born of Mary, God was present among his people once more, but in a much more intimate and direct way. Also, the Ark of the Covenant contained within it the Word of God written on stone: the tablets of the Ten Commandments. When Mary carried the child Jesus in her womb, she too contained within her the Word of God, but in flesh rather than stone. Similarly, the Ark contained the bread from heaven, the manna that fed the Israelites in the Wilderness and which foreshadowed the Eucharist. And Mary held within her the true bread that came down from heaven (see Jn 6:48–50). Finally, the Ark carried the rod of Aaron, the symbol of the high priesthood. And Mary carried the true High Priest, Jesus (Heb 4:14).

The Head of the Madonna. Francesco di Cristofano (1485-1525)

Lesson 6

🎥 WHAT WE'LL COVER IN LESSON SIX

Marian Apparition: Our Lady of Lourdes

Themes Covered

» The nature and role of dogmas
» The dogma of Mary's Perpetual Virginity
» Mary's true interior, spiritual identity
» Old Testament foreshadows of Mary's perpetual virginity
» Answers to the objection of Jesus' "brethren"
» St. Jerome's answers to the claim Mary and Joseph had sexual relations after the birth of Jesus

Song of the Angels. William Bouguereau (1825-1905)

NOTES

"The world being unworthy to receive the Son of God directly from the hands of the Father, he gave his Son to Mary for the world to receive him from her."
— Saint Augustine —
(as quoted in *True Devotion to Mary*)

REVIEW QUESTIONS

1. What is a dogma?

2. Define the dogma of Mary's Perpetual Virginity.

3. How can Mary as the New Ark help to better understand her perpetual virginity?

4. How would you respond to the accusation that Mary must have had other children because the Gospels tell us Jesus was her "firstborn"? Or because they mention his "brethren"?

DISCUSSION QUESTIONS

1. Is the defining of dogmas restrictive to us as Christians? How is this role of the Magisterium helpful for us?

2. What do we mean when we say the Church's teachings about Mary tell us more about God than they tell us about her?

3. How can Mary and Joseph be the models of married life if Mary took a vow of perpetual virginity?

4. How is Mary's virginity not a rejection of the goodness of the marital act?

THIS LESSON'S MEMORY VERSE

"Behold, I am with you always, to the close of the age."
Matthew 28:20

PREPARATION FOR THE NEXT LESSON

» *Hail, Holy Queen,* Chapter 4
» Proverbs 31

Additional Study Resources Available at www.StPaulCenter.com

LESSON SEVEN

THE PROMISED MOTHER

The Holy Family. Pompeo Batoni (1708-1787)

The Niccolini-Cowper Madonna, detail. Raffaello Sanzio (1483-1520)

LESSON SEVEN

THE PROMISED MOTHER

※

REVIEW OF THE PREVIOUS LESSON

The Nature Of Dogmas

Broadly defined, a dogma is a truth pertaining to faith or morals that has been revealed by God, transmitted from the Apostles in the Scriptures or by Tradition, defined by the Church, and which the faithful are bound to believe. The Church's Magisterium—the pope and the bishops in union with him—has been entrusted by the Holy Spirit to preserve, protect, and proclaim God's revelation in the world. There are four of these dogmas: Mary's Immaculate Conception; Mary's title and role as "Mother of God"; Mary's Assumption into Heaven; and Mary's Perpetual Virginity.

Ever Virgin

The teaching of Mary's perpetual virginity is one of the longest defined dogmas of the Church. It was taught by the earliest Church Fathers, including: Tertullian, St. Athanasius, St. Ambrose, and St. Augustine. And it was officially declared a dogma at the Fifth Ecumenical Council in Constantinople in 553 A.D. That declaration called Mary "ever-virgin." A century later, a statement by Pope Martin I clarified that "ever-virgin" meant Mary was a virgin before, during, and after Christ's birth.

Of those three aspects of Mary's perpetual virginity, the easiest part to see in Scripture is her virginal conception of Christ. Both Matthew and Luke leave no room for doubt on that (Mt 1:18; Lk 1:34–35, 3:23). That virginal motherhood is the guarantor of both Jesus' divinity and Jesus' humanity. It safeguards the truth that he was both fully God and fully man.

Mary's Identity

Less apparent is Mary's virginity during and after Christ's birth. Understanding the reason for that first requires recognition that Mary's virginity wasn't just one attribute of hers among many. It's central to her identity. It's who she is. Not just biologically, but spiritually, interiorly. All her life, Mary possessed an integrity that every other human person since Adam and Eve has lacked. Because of that integrity, her body perfectly expressed her spirit. There was no tension between the two. Accordingly, since Mary's soul was entirely consecrated to God, so too was her body. Her physical virginity was a perpetual sign of that consecration.

Mary's virginity keeps the physical sign of an interior reality intact. Doing that took a miracle, but no more of a miracle than it took for Jesus, after his resurrection, to enter the room where His disciples awaited Him even though the door was locked (Jn 20:19). That's also one of the reasons why Mary and Joseph refrained from normal marital relations. Her virginity was too central to her identity to do otherwise.

Old Testament Types

That centrality is foreshadowed in the two Old Testament "types" of Mary: The Virgin Eve and the Ark of the Covenant. The Ark's holiness stemmed from the presence of God within it. That presence made it so sacred that anyone who touched it died instantly (2 Sam 6:6–7). Mary, like the Ark, had been set apart from everything else in creation. She contained the presence of God within her, closed to everyone and everything else in this respect.

Jesus' "Brethren"

The bulk of arguments against Mary's perpetual virginity rest upon New Testament passages that refer to Jesus' brethren (Mk 6:3; Lk 2:7). The Hebrew word for "brother," however, is a far more inclusive word than its English counterpart: It means "cousin" as well as "male sibling." In fact, in ancient Hebrew and Aramaic (the language Jesus spoke), there is no word for cousin. To Jews of Jesus' time, one's cousin was one's brother. Likewise, the word "firstborn" raises no difficulties because it was a legal term in ancient Israel that applied to the child who "opened the womb." It applied to that child regardless of whether or not the mother bore more children afterwards.

Telling Time

Another common argument made against Mary's perpetual virginity is based on passages in the Bible that seem to imply that Mary and Joseph had sexual relations after Jesus' birth (Mt 1:18, 25). Those who cite those texts say that the use of the words "before" and "until" imply that Mary and Joseph did "know" each other after Jesus' birth. Those arguments were answered, however, about 1600 years ago by St. Jerome. He explained, "[Scripture] often uses a fixed time… to denote time without limitation, as when God by the mouth of the prophet says to certain persons, 'Even to your old age I am He'" (Is 46:4). Jerome then asked: "Will He cease to be God when they have grown old?" There are many more examples like that in Scripture (see Deut 34:5–6; Ps 123:2; Mt 28:20; and 1 Cor 15:23–26).

The Unspoken Assumption

What Scripture implies is that well before the angel Gabriel appeared to her, Mary had already made a vow or at least had the intention of perpetual virginity. When Gabriel broke the news to Mary that she would conceive a son, her response was, "How can this be, since I have no husband?" An equally good translation of that sentence is, "How can this be, since I know not man?" Either rendering of Mary's question makes no sense unless she intended to remain a virgin. At the time Gabriel came to her, Mary was already betrothed to Joseph, and any young woman in that state would know how she would conceive a son. But, judging by the question she asked, that seemed beyond the realm of possibility to Mary. The unspoken assumption behind her words is that Mary intended to remain a virgin from an early age.

Lesson 7

WHAT WE'LL COVER IN LESSON SEVEN

Marian Apparition: Our Lady of Pontmain (Our Lady of Hope)

Themes Covered:

- The wise advice of King Lemuel's mother
- The role of the *Gebirah*, or queen mother, in the Davidic kingdom
- The Old Testament prophecies of Isaiah and Micah regarding Our Lady
- Queen Mother Mary
- Mary's important place in Matthew's genealogy

Scripture Verses Read By Cardinal Donald Wuerl In This Lesson

- Proverbs 31:9
- 1 Kings 2:19
- 1 Kings 2:20–21
- Acts 2:25–36

Virgin and Child with St. Catherine of Alexandria. Anthony van Dyck (1599-1641)

NOTES

"Because the virgin Mary was raised to such a lofty dignity as to be the mother of the King of kings, it is deservedly and by every right that the Church has honored her with the title of 'Queen'."
— St. Alphonsus Ligouri —

Lesson 7

REVIEW QUESTIONS

1. Where does the advice in Proverbs 31 originate? Why is this significant?

2. Who sits at the right hand of the kings of Israel?

3. What were the duties of Israel's Queen Mother?

4. What is significant about Isaiah's and Micah's prophecies of the future king?

DISCUSSION QUESTIONS

1. In the ancient Near East, references to the future king almost always mention the father. Why does this make sense? Why is this different for prophecies about Christ?

2. How is Bathsheba a foreshadowing of the Blessed Virgin Mary?

3. What can our culture learn from the importance of the Blessed Mother? Why or why not?

THIS LESSON'S MEMORY VERSE

"Behold, a virgin shall conceive and bear a Son, and his name shall be called Emmanuel (which means, God with us)."
Matthew 1:23

PREPARATION FOR THE NEXT LESSON

» *Hail, Holy Queen*, Review pages 99–102
» Matthew 2
» *Catechism of the Catholic Church* 466, 495, & 971

Additional Study Resources Available at www.StPaulCenter.com

LESSON EIGHT

MOTHER CROWNED IN GLORY

Madonna and Child, surrounded by St. John Baptist and two angels. Francesco Botticini (1446-1497)

The Niccolini-Cowper Madonna, detail. Raffaello Sanzio (1483-1520)

LESSON EIGHT
MOTHER CROWNED IN GLORY

REVIEW OF THE PREVIOUS LESSON

Wise Advice

One of the first things we hear about Solomon's reign is the important part his mother played in it. In 1 Kings 2:19–21, when Bathsheba enters her son's court, he bows to her. Then, he has her seated on a throne at his right hand. After Bathsheba takes her seat she acts in her traditional role as intercessor for the people. She puts a request made by one of Solomon's brothers before her son. Although Solomon told his mother he would grant her anything she asked, he actually doesn't this time around…which was a wise decision. His brother was asking to marry one of David's concubines, and in ancient Near Eastern cultures, marrying the king's concubine or wife was tantamount to declaring yourself king. What's important here, however, is not whether Solomon did as his mother asked. What's important is that he acknowledged her right to ask. By placing the Queen Mother in such an exalted position, Solomon shows his court that the Queen Mother has the right to intercede for others.

The *Gebirah*

After Solomon's death, the Queen Mother continued to be one of the distinctive features of the Davidic kingdom. In Jeremiah 13:18, God's instructions to Jeremiah begin: "Say to the king and the queen mother…" The prophecy of doom that follows would not have been addressed to both the king and his mother unless they were both powerful leaders in the kingdom. All through the history of the Davidic kingdom, the Queen Mother occupied a place second only to the king. In Hebrew, she was called *Gebirah*, meaning "Great Lady." Her duties included advising the king as no one else could and interceding for the people before the king. She also was a visible sign of the king's legitimate rule. That's because she wasn't just the king's mother, she was also the former king's wife. Her motherhood of the king was a testimony to his descent from the previous king.

The Promised Mother

When God established His covenant with David, He promised the young king that his kingdom would last forever (2 Sam 7:16). But, when the kingdom collapsed some 400 years later, it seemed as if God had gone back on his promise. But God's promise was unconditional, and the Israelites believed the prophets who told of the day when the Kingdom of David would be restored. Those prophecies about the restoration of the kingdom, however, weren't just about the future King. They were also about his mother (Is 7:14, Mic 5:1–3). To the ancient Israelites that would have sounded very unusual. In the Bible (not to mention other ancient documents from the Near East) it is the father who figures prominently in any references to a son or a king. The mother is often not mentioned at all.

Like Isaiah and Micah, however, the writers of the Gospel draw attention to Jesus' mother, connecting both Him and her with the words of the prophets. For example, Matthew's Gospel begins with a genealogy of Jesus Christ.

And at the end of this genealogy we find Mary: "of whom Jesus was born, who is called Christ." Matthew's words recall the words of Isaiah and Micah: It's the mother who is emphasized. She is the one of whom the promised King is born. She is the Queen Mother foretold by the prophets. That point is reinforced by the other women on the list. Four women are named in Matthew's genealogy, and the last of those women before Mary is Bathsheba, the mother of Solomon. She was the prototypical Queen Mother, just as Solomon was the prototypical son of David.

Mother Crowned in Glory

🎬 WHAT WE'LL COVER IN LESSON EIGHT

Marian Apparition: Our Lady of Knock

Themes Covered

» Mary's royal title in the Gospels of Luke and John
» The dogma of Mary as Mother of God (*Theotokos*)
» How Mary's title as Mother of God protects the humanity and divinity of Jesus

Scripture Verses Read By Cardinal Donald Wuerl In This Lesson

» Matthew 2:1–12
» Luke 1:31–33
» Luke 1:43

The Coronation of the Virgin. Annibale Carracci (1560-1609)

NOTES

"Let us not imagine that we obscure the glory of the Son by the great praise we lavish on the Mother; for the more she is honored, the greater is the glory of her Son. There can be no doubt that whatever we say in praise of the Mother gives equal praise to the Son."
— Saint Bernard of Clairvaux —

REVIEW QUESTIONS

1. What are some details in the Gospels that point to Mary being the Queen Mother?

2. What was the first official Marian dogma defined by the Church?

3. What scriptural precedent is there for the title "Mother of God"?

4. What controversy in the early Church was behind the debate over Mary's title, "Mother of God"?

5. Where and how was that controversy settled?

DISCUSSION QUESTIONS

1. Why do you think the vast majority of early Christians had no objections to the title? What does their acceptance of that title teach us?

2. How does recognizing that Mary is the Queen Mother of her Son's Kingdom change your understanding of how you can relate to her?

3. Why do you think many non-Catholics object to Mary's title, "Mother of God"?

4. Have you ever found yourself sympathetic to their objections? Why or why not?

THIS LESSON'S MEMORY VERSE

> "And why is this granted me, that the mother of my Lord should come to me?"
> Luke 1:43

PREPARATION FOR THE NEXT LESSON

- *Hail, Holy Queen*, Review pages 94–98
- Genesis 3:15–19
- *Catechism of the Catholic Church* 490, 722, & 2676

Additional Study Resources Available at www.StPaulCenter.com

LESSON NINE

FULL OF GRACE

The Annunciation. Leonardo da Vinci (1452-1519)

The Niccolini-Cowper Madonna, detail. Raffaello Sanzio (1483-1520)

LESSON NINE

FULL OF GRACE

※

REVIEW OF THE PREVIOUS LESSON

Holding Court

Matthew takes up this idea of a royal mother in the second chapter of his Gospel (v. 1–12). In that passage, we see three visitors who have traveled across the desert to see the newborn "king of the Jews." When they arrive, they find "the child with Mary his mother." Appropriately, these visitors come bearing gifts, much as the visitors to Solomon's court would have: gold, frankincense, and myrrh. Gold and spices were tributes regularly paid to Solomon by royal visitors (1 Kgs 10:10, 25). And the only other times in Scripture when myrrh and frankincense are mentioned together are in the Song of Solomon, when they are part of the pageantry of Solomon's wedding day (See Songs 3:6–7, 11).

A Royal Title

Luke also depicts Mary as the Queen Mother. At the Annunciation, the angel Gabriel tells Mary she will give birth to a royal Son who will rule from the throne of David (1:31–33). A few verses later, Luke shows Elizabeth recognizing Mary as the Queen Mother (1:43). The title she uses—"mother of my Lord"— is full of queenly significance. In ancient Israel, the king was addressed as "my Lord" (2 Sam 24:21), which would make the Queen Mother the "mother of my Lord."

The final glimpse of the Queen Mother in the Bible comes in John's Revelation, chapter 12, the famous symbolic vision of a woman. There we find Mary, the Queen Mother enthroned in heaven with her Son, the King.

Lesson 9

Mother of God

The image of Mary as Queen Mother is directly related to the first official Marian dogma defined by the Church: Mary's status as Mother of God. The Greek word for the title is *Theotokos*, which literally means "God-bearer." That title is one of the oldest and most commonly used titles for Mary, with Christians using it in the very first centuries of the Church. The title also appears in one of the oldest known Christian prayers, the *Sub Tuum Praesidium* ("Beneath Your Protection"), an early form of the *Memorare* that dates to the third century.

The first Christians called Mary the "Mother of God" without hesitation. There was scriptural precedent, and it seemed logical. If Jesus was God, and Mary was his mother, then that made her the Mother of God. That sort of logic depends on a principle called the "Communication of Idioms." According to that principle, whatever one says about either of Christ's natures can be truly said of Christ himself. That's because His two natures, the divine nature and the human nature, were united in Him. He is one divine person.

The Contest Begins

In the fifth century, however, some people raised the same objections to the title that many non-Catholics raise today: They argued that the title "Mother of God" implied that Mary was the "originator of God." Those objectors said that they could accept the title "Mother of Christ," but not "Mother of God." At the heart of those objections, however, was an objection to the unity of Christ's two natures. Mary, they claimed, gave birth only to Christ's human nature, not his divine nature. The Church, led by Pope Celestine I and St. Cyril of Alexandria, disagreed. As St. Cyril pointed out, a mother gives birth to a person, not a nature. Accordingly, Mary gave birth to Jesus Christ, who was and is a divine person. Although Mary did not "originate" or "generate" God, she did bear Him in her womb and give birth to Him. She was God's mother.

The Heart Of The Matter

The controversy over Mary's title as "Mother of God" was addressed in 431 A.D. at the Council of Ephesus. There, more was at stake than simply defending Mary's title. The Christian teaching about Christ's two natures was the real issue. The Church wanted to settle one question: Was Jesus one person or two? Rejecting the teaching of the heretic Nestorius, the Church declared that Jesus is one divine person, with two natures—his mother's human nature and his Father's divine nature. Mary did not give Jesus his divine nature or his divine personhood—those He possessed from all eternity as the only begotten Son of the Father. But she also didn't just give Him His flesh: She gave birth to the whole person. She gave birth to Jesus Christ, both God and man. That is what we confess every time we say the Apostles' Creed.

Guarding Truth

Calling Mary "Mother of God" states a truth that must be stated in order to protect an essential truth about Christ. In a similar way, that's what all Mary's queenly predecessors did for their sons. One of the three essential tasks of the Queen Mother was to be a sign of her son's legitimacy. She was the link between his father, the former rightful king, and her son, the present rightful king. Likewise, Mary as the virginal "Mother of God" is the link between her Son's humanity and divinity. She is the sign that He is both God and man.

Rest on the Flight into Egypt. Bartolomé Esteban Murillo (1617-1682)

Lesson 9

📽 WHAT WE'LL COVER IN LESSON NINE

Marian Apparition: Our Lady of Fátima

Themes Covered

- Definition of the dogma of the Immaculate Conception
- The connection between the "first gospel" (Genesis 3:15), Revelation 12, and the Immaculate Conception
- The total opposition between Mary and Satan
- How the Annunciation account in Luke supports Mary's Immaculate Conception

Scripture Verses Read By Cardinal Donald Wuerl In This Lesson

- Genesis 3:15
- Genesis 3:16–19
- Romans 5:12
- Luke 1:28

Immaculate Conception. Francisco de Zurbarán (1597-1664)

NOTES

"Mary, who is the Virgin most pure, is also the refuge of sinners. She knows what sin is – not by the experience of its fall, not by tasting its bitter regrets, but by seeing what it did to her Divine Son."
— Archbishop Fulton J. Sheen —
(*Victory Over Vice*)

REVIEW QUESTIONS

1. Define the dogma of the Immaculate Conception. What three Scripture passages support this dogma?

2. Why is Genesis 3:15 known as the "first gospel"? How does the "first gospel" form part of the biblical foundation of the dogma of the Immaculate Conception?

3. What does the Greek word *kecharitoméne* mean? How does the story of the Annunciation form part of the biblical foundation of the dogma of the Immaculate Conception?

DISCUSSION QUESTIONS

1. Had you previously understood the full power of the word "enmity"? How does that help us to understand the Immaculate Conception?

2. Why do you think it was important that Jesus' mother be free from the stain of sin? What did her Immaculate Conception make possible?

3. How can Mary be our model if she was conceived without sin?

THIS LESSON'S MEMORY VERSE

> "Hail, full of grace, the Lord is with thee!"
> Luke 1:28

Lesson 9

PREPARATION FOR THE NEXT LESSON

» Romans 3:19–31
» *Catechism of the Catholic Church* 491–493

Additional Study Resources Available at www.StPaulCenter.com

LESSON TEN

ALL HOLY

Virgin & Child in Clouds. Bartolomé Esteban Murillo (1617-1682)

The Niccolini-Cowper Madonna, detail. Raffaello Sanzio (1483-1520)

LESSON TEN

ALL HOLY

☙

REVIEW OF PREVIOUS LESSON

The Immaculate Conception

The dogma of the Immaculate Conception states that in God's plan and by His grace, Mary was kept free from sin from the moment of her conception until the end of her earthly life. Not only was she free from sin, but she was also free from concupiscence, the disordered desires which lead to sin. Catholics have believed that since the earliest days of the Church. But, although the Church's saints and doctors had written about Mary's Immaculate Conception for centuries, the teaching did not become an official dogma until 1854, when Pope Pius IX declared the teaching in a document entitled *Ineffabilis Deus* ("The Ineffable God").

In addition to the fact the Church had long believed Mary was unstained by Original Sin, Pius IX also pointed out that this belief was founded on three passages from Scripture: The "first gospel" in the Garden of Eden (Gen 3:15); the Annunciation (Lk 1:26–38); and the vision of the "woman" in Revelation 12.

The First Gospel

Genesis 3:15 is the inaugural announcement of the salvation that would come from a woman and her offspring. In that "first gospel" God promised that there would be perpetual enmity between this woman and the serpent.

Remember that it is God who establishes the enmity. This enmity is a divinely created opposition, one God established for all time. Moreover, this enmity is two-fold: It's between the serpent and the woman, and between the serpent's offspring and the woman's offspring. The woman's offspring will crush the head of the serpent (i.e. kill it).

From a close reading, we can see why the Church—beginning in the New Testament —has long believed that this text is evidence of Mary's Immaculate Conception. First, it foresees a new "woman" (a New Eve), and her "seed," in mortal combat with a serpent. We learn from Revelation 12—which is a dramatic portrayal of the conflict promised in Genesis 3—that the serpent is Satan (Rev 12:9). Revelation 12 is also where we learn that the offspring of the woman is both Jesus and "those who keep the commandments of God and bear testimony to Jesus" (Rev 12:5; Rev 12:17). And, accordingly, it's where we learn that the woman is a symbol for Mary, the mother of Jesus (Rev 12:5).

From Scripture To Dogma

Remember, in the Garden of Eden, after God promised a Redeemer who would crush the serpent, He told Adam and Eve what their punishment would be (Gen 3:16–19). That punishment, however, didn't just apply to Adam and Eve. It applies to all men and women. But the *proto-evangelium* also seems to envision at least two people—the woman and her offspring—to whom that punishment will not apply. Those two people will not be conceived under the rule of the serpent and the consequences of the serpent's deceit. The woman and the serpent will be engaged in a mortal rivalry, a hatred that implies a struggle to the death. How could Mary live in absolute opposition to the serpent (the devil), and still be under his power? She couldn't. If Mary was conceived with original sin, there couldn't be the perpetual enmity promised by God between the woman and the serpent. To the contrary, if Mary was conceived with original sin, the serpent would be victorious, subjecting the woman to his power, and God's promise would be false.

Full Of Grace

Evidence of Mary's sinless state exists in the very first sentence of the Annunciation account in Luke, as well (Lk 1:28). This is a greeting found nowhere else in Scripture. The word that's translated as "favored one" or "full of grace" is *kecharitoméne*, a form of the verb *charitoo*. That's an extremely rare verb, used only in the Annunciation scene and in Paul's letter to the Ephesians. In each case, it indicates an action that causes some effect in the object of the verb.

In Luke, the tense of this verb in the angel's address implies that Mary has already been favored by the bestowal of God's grace. The sense of the passage is that Mary has already been graced, she is graced now, and will continue to be "full of grace."

The Annunciation. Nicolas Poussin (1594-1665)

Lesson 10

WHAT WE'LL COVER IN LESSON TEN

Marian Apparition: Our Lady of Beauraing (Virgin of the Golden Heart)

Themes Covered

» Mary's new name
» God's fitting reason for Mary's Immaculate Conception
» The response to common objections regarding the Immaculate Conception

Scripture Verses Read By Cardinal Donald Wuerl In This Lesson

» Romans 3:20–23

Virgin and Child with Angels. Bartolomeo Cavarozzi (1587-1625)

NOTES

"Mary's greatness consists in the fact that she wants to magnify God, not herself."
— Pope Benedict XVI —
(*Deus Caritas Est*)

REVIEW QUESTIONS

1. How does the dogma of the Immaculate Conception reveal truths about Christ?

2. What would you say if someone claimed the dogma of the Immaculate Conception meant Mary didn't need a Savior?

3. Why does Romans 3:20–23 not disprove Mary's Immaculate Conception?

DISCUSSION QUESTIONS

1. Mary was preserved from sin entirely, but many of us are also preserved from sin in lesser ways. How has God preserved you from certain sins?

2. How does Mary's Immaculate Conception increase, not decrease, Jesus' glory?

3. Why do you think the liturgy calls the Blessed Mother a sign of the Church and a "promise of its perfection"?

THIS LESSON'S MEMORY VERSE

> "Blessed be the God and Father of our Lord Jesus Christ, who has blessed us in Christ with every spiritual blessing in the heavenly places, even as he chose us in him before the foundation of the world, that we should be holy and blameless before him."
> Ephesians 1:3-4

PREPARATION FOR THE NEXT LESSON

» *Hail, Holy Queen*, Review pages 107–113
» *Catechism of the Catholic Church* 966

Additional Study Resources Available at www.StPaulCenter.com

LESSON ELEVEN

THE ASSUMPTION

Assumption of the Virgin. Guido Reni (1575-1642)

The Niccolini-Cowper Madonna, detail. Raffaello Sanzio (1483-1520)

LESSON ELEVEN

THE ASSUMPTION

❧

REVIEW OF PREVIOUS LESSON

What's In A Name?

At the Annunciation, Gabriel doesn't call Mary by name. Instead he calls her "full of grace." No other person in all of Scripture is addressed this way by an angel. It's almost as if "Full of Grace" were Mary's name. Throughout Scripture, when God gives a person a new name, it indicates that person's true place in God's plan of salvation (Gen 17:5, 32:28, 35:10–11; Mt 16:18). Likewise, when we hear Mary called "full of grace," that signals to us something about her role in salvation history. In her name, her destiny is revealed.

Fitting

There is clear evidence in Scripture for Mary's Immaculate Conception, but why did God preserve Mary from the lot of the rest of us? Because it was fitting. God thought it appropriate for Jesus to inherit a sinless human nature from His mother, just as he inherited her eyes and her nose and skin color. Likewise, just as the priest takes the greatest care to purify the sacred vessels used in the Mass, the vessels which contain the Eucharistic Body and Blood of Jesus, so too did God take great care to purify the vessel which would carry the flesh and blood of Jesus in her womb and care for Him all his life.

Lesson 11

Common Objections

Despite the Scriptural proofs and logic in favor of the Immaculate Conception, the dogma has long been one of the most contested of the Church's teachings. The most common concern is that in saying Mary is sinless or all-holy, we are somehow making her more than human or making Christ's saving work less important. But in the very document that declared the dogma of the Immaculate Conception, "The Ineffable God," Pope Pius IX made it clear that the Immaculate Conception is a "singular grace" of God and that that grace was won for her by Jesus Christ. Jesus was her savior, just as He was the savior for the rest of the human race. Finally, he says that Mary's Immaculate Conception was a divine act of preservation. It was a work of God and not a work of Mary herself.

The Immaculate Conception, then, was a fruit of the redemption applied to Mary by way of anticipation. God is not bound by time like us. This is how Christ's death on Calvary could obtain the fruit of salvation for those who had died hundreds of years before Him and those who would not be born until almost 2,000 years after His death. Just as we have been redeemed by a God who died on a cross long before we were born, so too was Mary saved, at the moment of her conception, by a God who had not yet been born in time, a God whose saving death was still years away. She needed a savior. She needed to be redeemed, just like the rest of us. But her redemption was an act of preservation, whereas others' redemption was an act of deliverance.

Another common objection, frequently voiced by non-Catholics, is this: How can the Church claim that Mary was sinless, when Scripture itself states that "all have sinned"? (Rom 3:23). In that section of Romans, however, Paul is talking about the sinfulness of Jews and Gentiles. He makes the argument that the mere act of being Jewish does not make a person holier or more virtuous. He also argues that strict adherence to the Mosaic law cannot give life. Paul compares groups, not individuals. And when he talks about "all men" he's talking about all races of men. If by "all men" Paul really meant every single individual person ever conceived, he would be accusing Jesus of sin, not to mention babies and the unborn.

The Assumption

🎬 WHAT WE'LL COVER IN LESSON ELEVEN

Marian Apparition: Our Lady of Banneux (Our Lady of the Poor)

Themes Covered

- The dogma of the Assumption
- John's vision of "the woman clothed with the sun" in Revelation 12
- Old Testament imagery in Revelation identifying Mary as Daughter Zion, the Queen-Bride of Israel, and the Mother of the Church
- The fulfillment of the "first gospel" in the battle of Revelation 12
- More Old Testament foreshadows of Mary's Assumption

Scripture Verses Read By Cardinal Donald Wuerl In This Lesson

- Revelation 11:19–12:1
- Exodus 19:16–17
- Revelation 11:15–19
- Isaiah 7:10–11; 14
- Isaiah 60:19–20
- Isaiah 60:3–5
- Revelation 12:3–17
- John 14:1–3

Madonna del Popolo. Federico Barocci (1535-1612)

NOTES

"Never be afraid of loving the Blessed Virgin too much.
You can never love her more than Jesus did."
— Saint Maximilian Kolbe —

REVIEW QUESTIONS

1. Define the dogma of the Assumption.

2. How does the appearance of the Ark in Revelation parallel the theophany—the visible manifestation of God's presence—of Exodus? What other Old Testament scenes does the appearance of the Ark recall?

3. How is Revelation 12 a fulfillment of Genesis 3?

4. How do the Old Testament types help us to understand Mary's Assumption?

Lesson 11

DISCUSSION QUESTIONS

1. Which Old Testament type of the Blessed Mother is your favorite? How does that type tell you something about her and her role in salvation history?

2. Some say the woman in Revelation 12 represents Israel; others say it is Mary. How can both be right?

3. How does the battle of Revelation 12 continue today? Do you call on the Blessed Mother for help?

The Assumption

THIS LESSON'S MEMORY VERSE

> "Then God's temple in heaven was opened, and the ark of the covenant was seen within his temple; and there were flashes of lightning, voices, peals of thunder, an earthquake, and heavy hail. And a great portent appeared in heaven, a woman clothed with the sun, with the moon under her feet, and on her head a crown of twelve stars."
> Revelation 11:19–12:2

PREPARATION FOR THE NEXT LESSON

» *Hail, Holy Queen*, Chapter 6
» *Catechism of the Catholic Church* 967–972

Additional Study Resources Available at www.StPaulCenter.com

LESSON TWELVE

ALWAYS A MOTHER

Madonna & Child III. Giovanni Battista Salvi ('Sassoferrato', 1605-1685)

The Niccolini-Cowper Madonna, detail. Raffaello Sanzio (1483-1520)

LESSON TWELVE
ALWAYS A MOTHER

※

REVIEW OF PREVIOUS LESSON

The Assumption

The dogma of the Assumption teaches that at the end of her time on earth, Mary was taken up—body and soul—into heaven. There, she sits at her Son's right hand, as Queen of Heaven and Earth. The foundation for the teaching is rooted in Scripture, specifically in John's mysterious and apocalyptic vision recorded in Revelation 12.

The Ark Returns

After hiding the Ark of the Covenant around 586 B.C. (2 Macc 2:4–8), Jeremiah foretold that the Ark would remain hidden until the time when "God gathers his people together again and shows his mercy." The prophets envisioned this restoration as a great in-gathering of Israel's exiles (See 2 Macc 2:18; Is 11:12, 15–16; Jer 31:8–10; Ezek 36:25; 37:21, 38:8–12). When prophesying about the return of the Ark, Jeremiah alluded to the first exodus, led by Moses, as well as to the kingdom and temple. He promised that the "glory of the Lord" would be seen in a cloud—which is how God's presence came to the tabernacle in the time of Moses and how it came to the temple in the time of Solomon (see Ex 40:34–35; 1 Kgs 8:11).

The Ark Revealed

All those images Jeremiah used and all the expectations for the people of God that he talked about, are realized in the Book of Revelation. This starts with John's vision of the Ark, which deliberately evokes the "theophany" or appearance of God to Moses on Mount Sinai (Ex 19:16–17) and the Old Testament story depicting the fall of Jericho (see Josh 6:1–20). What John shows us with this imagery is that the time for the fulfillment of Jeremiah's prophecy—and the promise of a new exodus for Israel—has come. Christ is risen. The Kingdom has been restored. And the Ark can be revealed. And when the Ark is revealed, it's revealed as a woman. But not just any ordinary woman. Her identity is multi-faceted.

Daughter Zion, Queen-Bride, Mother Of The Church

First and foremost, the woman of Revelation 12 is identified as Mary, the one "who brought forth a male child, one who is to rule all the nations with a rod of iron…[the one] caught up to God and his throne" (Rev 12:5). Revelation 12, however, also uses imagery that reveals the woman to be Daughter Zion, the Queen-Bride of Israel, and the Mother of the Church.

In likening the woman to the Queen Bride of Israel, his description of her echoes Isaiah, who said that Israel would be arrayed like a radiant Queen Bride (Is 60:19–20, 62:3–5). Solomon's bride in the Song of Solomon is similarly described (Songs 6:10). John drives this point home by telling us that the woman wears a crown of twelve stars, an obvious symbol of the twelve tribes of Israel.

But, throughout Revelation, the twelve tribes are also reckoned as signs of the twelve Apostles, the representatives of the new Israel, the Church (Rev 7:4–8, 21:12–14). So, just as Daughter Zion was a symbol of the chosen people of God—Israel—the woman in Revelation is also a symbol of the new people of God, the Church. Paul, in language similar to that of Revelation, called the Church "the Jerusalem above…our mother." He also spoke of the Church as the Bride of Christ (Gal 4:26; Eph 5:31–32). Likewise, John referred to the Church as a "Lady" (2 Jn, v. 5). The woman of Revelation, however, is more than a symbol for the Church. She is also its mother with "offspring" in addition to the one male child to whom she gives birth. And those children are described in Revelation as those who believe in Jesus.

The First Gospel Fulfilled

In Revelation 12 we see a great battle which is a dramatic portrayal of the fulfillment of God's promise in the Garden of Eden. The serpent lies in wait beneath the woman, preparing to devour her offspring. The birth of her son becomes the occasion for mortal combat. During the battle, the woman flees into the desert—to a place especially prepared for her by God. Later, after the devil's defeat, John sees the woman given eagle's wings to fly to a place in the desert where she would be nourished by God. John's language recalls Jesus' words to his Apostles in John 14:1–3. The language of preparing a place is also often used in the New Testament to describe the destiny God has planned for his children (Mt 20:23, 25:34; 1 Pet 1:5; 1 Cor 2:9). John's words also evoke God's care for Israel in the wilderness (Ex 19:4; Deut 1:31–33, 32:10–12, 8:2–3).

Connecting The Dots

The picture Revelation paints serves as the biblical outline for the Church's dogma of Mary's Assumption. Mary is Daughter Zion, the woman who gave birth to the world's Savior. Because she is the New Eve, she is free from the shadow of sin and its consequences. This includes the long-term separation of soul and body that exists for the rest of us as we wait for the resurrection of the body at the end of time. Mary has been taken up into heaven by God to join her Son in the place He prepared for her. And in that place, as Christ the King's mother, she sits at His right hand, wearing the crown of the Queen Mother. Additional scriptural evidence for Mary's Assumption lies in the fact that there are at least two foreshadowings of it in the Old Testament as seen with Enoch and Elijah.

Assumption of the Virgin. Annibale Carracci (1560-1609)

Lesson 12

🎥 WHAT WE'LL COVER IN LESSON TWELVE

The Marian Papacy of St. John Paul II

Themes Covered

- » The early witness of the Church to the Assumption
- » The celebration of the Assumption in the liturgy
- » Mary's role as Queen of Heaven
- » Mary as Christ's ultimate co-worker: Co-redemptrix, Mediatrix, and Advocate
- » Our honor and veneration of Mary our Mother

Scripture Verses Read By Cardinal Donald Wuerl In This Lesson

- » 1 Kings 2:19

The Assumption of the Virgin. Tiziano Vecelli ('Titian', 1488-1576)

NOTES

"To recite the Rosary is nothing other than to contemplate the face of Christ with Mary."
— Pope St. John Paul II —
(*Rosarium Virginis Mariae*)

Lesson 12

REVIEW QUESTIONS

1. What are some of the arguments from Church history and Tradition that point to the truth of Mary's Assumption?

2. What are Mary's duties as Queen of Heaven and Earth? How do these duties correspond to the duties of the Queen Mother of Israel?

3. How is the Rosary scriptural?

4. What is the response to someone accusing Catholics of worshipping Mary?

DISCUSSION QUESTIONS

1. What are some of the ways that you show your love for Christ's mother? What more can you do to show that love?

2. What do you think showing love for and honoring Christ's mother "does" for you? How does it bring you closer to Christ? Why does it do this?

3. In what ways are you a fellow worker of Christ's and a mediator of His love, grace, and truth to the world? What does your ability to do that tell you about Mary's ability to do likewise?

4. Has your understanding of any of our beliefs about Mary deepened during this study?

5. How can you honor the Blessed Mother more? How will you allow this study to impact your daily life?

THIS LESSON'S MEMORY VERSE

> "'O death, where is thy victory? O death, where is thy sting?' The sting of death is sin, and the power of sin is the law. But thanks be to God, who gives us the victory through our Lord Jesus Christ."
> 1 Corinthians 15:55–57

FOLLOW-UP READING

» *Hail, Holy Queen,* Chapters 7 & 8

Madonna of the Harpies. Andrea del Sarto (1486-1530)

LESSON 12 REVIEW NOTES

Munificentissimus Deus

Like the dogma of the Immaculate Conception, the dogma of the Assumption was officially declared relatively recently. It happened in 1950 when Pope Pius XII penned the apostolic constitution, *Munificentissimus Deus* ("The Most Bountiful God"). But, also like the Immaculate Conception, the dogma of the Assumption is nothing new. As far back as the fourth century, early Christians were writing about Mary's Assumption. And by the sixth century, there was a feast day established to commemorate the event. Although most of the writings we have from the early Church chronicle all the challenges made to the faith, there is no writing contesting Mary's Assumption. This indicates that no one was challenging the doctrine. Even more notably, during the period of the Church Fathers, no church or city ever claimed to possess the bones of Jesus' mother.

"God's Fellow Workers"

The Scriptures, Tradition, and the Church's Liturgy all illuminate the truth about Mary's Assumption into heaven. They also tell us that as the Queen Mother, Mary has the same responsibilities that Israel's Queen Mother had. What the Queen Mother did in Solomon's day and what Mary did at Cana is what Mary continues to do in heaven: She intercedes for her children. Always a mother, Mary watches over us, prays for us, and leads us ever closer to her Son. Because of that, you will sometimes hear the Church refer to her as our Co-redemptrix, Mediatrix, or Advocate, titles that identify her unique role in salvation history. Non-Catholics usually protest those titles, citing, for example, St. Paul's categorical assertion that Christ is the "one mediator between God and men" (1 Tm 2:5). St. Paul gives us some insight into how to reconcile those two statements when he writes in 1 Corinthians 3:9 that, "We are God's fellow workers." Christ doesn't need fellow workers, but because He wants to raise up mature sons and daughters, He makes us his co-workers. As Christ's fellow workers, we live according to His Word, we love others as we love Him, and we accept our crosses (Col 1:24).

As Christ's mother and co-worker *par excellence*, she helps Him mediate grace and salvation to the world, and regularly intercedes for us in heaven. From her "yes" to God when He asked her to bear his Son, to all the love and care she showed for Him in his lifetime, and to her final acceptance of His self-offering on the cross, Mary partnered with God in the work of our salvation in a unique way such that she can be called Co-redemptrix, Mediatrix, and Advocate without taking anything away from her Son's role as the "one mediator."

Hail Mary

Because Mary has done and continues to do so much for us, we honor and venerate her. We also ask for her intercession by praying prayers such as the *Memorare*, the "Hail Holy Queen," and, of course, the Rosary. Of all the different ways Catholics love and honor Mary, praying the Rosary is perhaps both the most common and the most important. It is a meditation on the life and work of Christ that engages the whole person on at least three levels, with the sounds of the voice, the feeling of the beads, and the sight of devotional images. In that way, all those senses can be brought into a spirit of prayer. Furthermore, the devotion itself is deeply scriptural. It includes prayers such as the "Our Father"(Mt 6:9–13), and the "Hail Mary," a prayer which originated in the words of the angel Gabriel at the Annunciation and the word's of Mary's cousin Elizabeth at the Visitation (Lk 1:28, 42). The Rosary also requires us to meditate on twenty different mysteries of the Gospel.

Our Mother

Catholics worship and adore only God. We do, however, honor and venerate Mary with great love and devotion because she so clearly manifests the grace of God, because she reminds us of what we're all called to be, because of the great part she played in helping bring about Christ's saving work, and because of the great part she continues to play in that work, praying and interceding for us in heaven. Above all, we honor her because she is our mother in faith, given to us by Christ as He hung upon the cross (Jn 19:26–27).

Additional Study Resources Available at www.StPaulCenter.com

APPENDIX

COMMON MARIAN PRAYERS

The Coronation of the Virgin. Diego Velazquez (1599-1660)

The Niccolini-Cowper Madonna, detail. Raffaello Sanzio (1483-1520)

APPENDIX
COMMON MARIAN PRAYERS

Hail Mary

Hail Mary,

Full of grace,

The Lord is with Thee.

Blessed art Thou amongst women,

And blessed is the fruit

Of thy womb, Jesus.

Holy Mary,

Mother of God,

Pray for us sinners now,

And at the hour of our death. Amen.

The Visitation. Jeronimo Ezquerra (1660-1737)

Hail Holy Queen

Hail, Holy Queen, Mother of mercy,

Our life, our sweetness and our hope.

To thee do we cry, poor banished children of Eve:

To thee do we send up our sighs,

Mourning and weeping in this valley of tears.

Turn then, most gracious advocate,

Thine eyes of mercy toward us,

And after this our exile,

Show unto us the blessed fruit of thy womb, Jesus.

O clement, O loving, O sweet Virgin Mary!

v. Pray for us, O Holy Mother of God.

r. That we may be made worthy of the promises of Christ.

Amen.

Coronation of the Virgin with Saints. Joseph and Francis of Assisi Giulio Cesare Procaccini (1574-1625)

Memorare

Remember, O most gracious Virgin Mary,

That never was it known

That any one who fled to thy protection,

Implored thy help

Or sought thine intercession,

was left unaided.

Inspired by this confidence,

I fly unto thee, O Virgin of Virgins my Mother;

To thee do I come, before thee I stand, sinful and sorrowful;

O Mother of the Word incarnate,

Despise not my petitions,

But in thy mercy hear and answer me. Amen.

Immaculate Conception- Escorial. Bartolomé Esteban Murillo (1617-1682)

Journey Through Scripture

Sub Tuum Praesidium (Beneath Your Protection)

We fly to your patronage

Oh Holy Mother of God.

Despise not our petitions

In our necessities,

But deliver us from all dangers,

Oh ever glorious and blessed Virgin. Amen.

Our Lady of Grace and the Grand Masters of Montesa. Antoni Peris (1365-1436)

The *Angelus*

V- The Angel of the Lord declared unto Mary.

R- And she conceived by the Holy Spirit.

(Hail Mary....)

V- Behold the handmaid of the Lord.

R- Be it done unto me according to thy word.

(Hail Mary....)

V- And the Word was made flesh.

R- And dwelt among us.

(Hail Mary....)

V- Pray for us, O Holy Mother Of God.

R- That we may be made worthy of the promises of Christ.

V- Let us pray:

R- Pour forth, we beseech Thee, O Lord, Thy grace into our hearts;

That, we to whom the incarnation of Christ, Thy Son,

Was made known by the message of an angel,

May by His passion and cross,

Be brought to the glory of His resurrection

Through the same Christ our Lord. Amen.

The Annunciation. Francisco de Zurbarán (1597-1664)

VISIT JOURNEYTHROUGHSCRIPTURE.COM
TO ORDER *HAIL, HOLY QUEEN*

Cover: Madonna of the Magnificat by Sandro Botticelli